AF572531

# MORTAL COMPANIONS

*CHARLES FISHMAN*

PLEASURE DOME PRESS LONG ISLAND 1977

ACKNOWLEDGMENTS: some of the poems in this book have been published in the following periodicals: "November, 1970" in *Bulletin of Concerned Asian Scholars* (as "For the Living"); "A Refusal to Enter My Father's Skull" in *Cottonwood Review*; "Fantasy Over My Child's Tears" in *Descant*; "Song for the Relief Copters" in *Green's Magazine*; "Little Sister" in *Hand Book*; "A Morning at Dachau" in *Jewish Frontier*; "Spectrum Elegy" and "The Commuter" in *Journal 31*; "To Amy on Ward 10W" in *Juice*; "Old Women" and "A History Lesson" in *The Malahat Review*; "The Spider Dances" in *The New Infinity Review*; "The Firetruck" in *New York Quarterly*; "Dust for Beetles" in *Poet Lore*; "The Ice Poets" in *Process*; "Bungalow People" in *Road Apple Review*; "Death March" and "Big Sister" in *Samisdat*; "Anima" in *Tree*; "August 12, 1952" in *Wascana Review*; "A Dead Woman on the Subway" in *Xanadu*. "Naomi Ades (Age 3) Falls Out a Window and Sees an Angel" and "Bronx '47" were first printed in *Aurora* (Tree Books, Berkeley, 1974).

LIBRARY OF CONGRESS CATALOGING IN PUBLICATION DATA

Fishman, Charles.
Mortal Companions.

Poems.
I. Title

ISBN 0-918870-03-8 ltd. 77-76613
ISBN 0-918870-02-X
ISBN 0-918870-01-1 pbk.

*for my mother and father*

# CONTENTS

# *MORTAL COMPANIONS*

*They say the fit survive,*
*But I invoke the spirits of the lost.*
*Those that have not survived, the darkly lost,*
*To bring their meaning back into life again. . . .*
*—D. H. Lawrence, "Cypresses"*

## *SURVIVORS*

*They sleep in their houses*
*unconscious as doorposts*
*that stand before houses*

*that draw back from sidewalks*
*like dreamers who stumble*
*while walking on sidewalks*

*where sleepers are waking*
*like windows in houses*
*whose children are waking*

*and marching toward hallways*
*like gateways in graveyards*
*that mushroom in hallways*

*where mothers and fathers*
*with magical passwords*
*remember their fathers*

*who died under streetlamps*
*that stood before houses*
*where gangs shatter streetlamps*

*and switchblades leap open*
*like eyelids in faces*
*that dream that they sleep*

# NAOMI ADES (AGE 3) FALLS OUT A WINDOW AND SEES AN ANGEL

A story.
No. 17 in the repertoire:
*I ran upstairs and there—*
*with gold shining wings:*
*an angel!*
A vision.
But what did my mother see
floating in the stale yellowed voids
of Boston Road?
More than a ghost!
More than the Head Rabbi of Minsk!
Or was it Grandma's Friday Night Chicken
or the fat droplets and swirls
in the yellow soup
or the aurora of the candles
flickering in the twin worlds
of table linen and window?
A daylight vision.
Visitation.
The stones trapped in the walls
of the building
                    *the angel!*
the loose gray wallpapery dresses
of *her* mama
                  *the angel!*
the wet spot in the plaster
                              *the angel!*

the corridors stuffed with oily darkness
*the angel!*
the white paint on the iron ladder
disappearing into the ceiling
*the angel!*
the coaltruck
*the angel!*
the silver chute
*the angel!*
the bin.
The vanishing thunder
with gold shining wings!

*

Angels and angels.
Swedenborg's. Blake's.
Jacob's intransigent one.
Mohammed's. Buddha's
in the flesh of a deer.
Of light. Of darkness.
Of death.
Angels and angels.

*

*I ran upstairs and there—*

waiting for me,
floating over the banister—
you opened your Maupassant purse

and brought forth a cow's ear
an 8th-grade diploma in flames
like a prayer shawl in a bombed temple
a girlhood scented and vulnerable
as a meadow
and the mausoleum of Adonai

I opened the black gate
slept on the altar:
you held the knife
as it sliced under my nipple
seeking an angel of the Lord

*I believe you, Mama!*

*

Naomi Ades, the Doll of Boston Road,
spoiled till the childhood soured
and brought forth a woman
a mother    a wife:

Where is the magic window now, Mama?

I have danced to see you beautiful
I have danced to see you free
I have danced to see you in love with life

Always the angel, your fingers reaching
for golden wings

## BRONX '47

War over: no memory of war
                    no memory of little sister
                              chewing brown hair
2 years *before television*
                    listening behind closed doors
                    awed by extraterran contrails
                              under closed lids
(when I opened my eyes not one would
                              disappear)
Year of deep snow     fantasies of my body
vaulting over White Castle like Bellerophon
manic and invisible     lying down iced
and naked in the fish market
                              my arms buried
                              up to the wrist
                                        in sawdust
like Hasidic dancers up to their souls
                                        in trance
                    lost in the night gliding
                              with pigeons   white
                              flight feathers fanned
                                        open
the wind  iridescent  brotherly—
someone's attenuated trembling wand
                              extended indefinitely
                              into the air
Summer in the false country of New Jersey:
                              cow-udder warm

mornings thick<br>
with pollen<br>
lazing back into the cool water bed<br>
of the earth<br>
City nights, a density of life:<br>
*GAS HEATS BEST* against<br>
a gray sky<br>
under it, stoop ball against concrete . . .<br>
growing up or at least *older*—short pants<br>
king of Wheeler Avenue<br>
morning glories opening<br>
inside my hands<br>
chalking fences: *I HATE YOU! I LOVE YOU!*<br>
*WORLD!*

## BIG SISTER

You would lay me
back
and carefully
touch me,
touch me as if
I were a cow's
belly:
feeling too interested,
too tender,
keeping too long at it,
too surely

I remember you floating
above me
warmly,
your lips pressed wetly,
your breasts softly

Your hands burrowed
toward the center
of my body,
strong enough to raise
the dead

Childless and stunned,
you held me tightly,

and I would pull you
more deeply
into needing me,
drawing your mouth
downwards, slowly

## LITTLE SISTER

In one black hole
my mother with my
father, snoring.
In a second hole
my sister, sleeping
sound. Down the dark
corridor
between them, I
am moving, the night
a slow bleeding,
my nostrils dark moons
of space, the walls
flickering
with their own solemn
life, the silence aching
in my feet in the deep
ening snow drifts in this
tunnel
beneath the world.

## BUDDY'S DEATH

Old bleak black humped-over Dodge
still as a basking tortoise:
inside, limp in the cracked-straw seats,
we're waiting: still as bugs on a slide,
sliding downhill into baked jelly sun

        Buddy is dying
                        his taut white
        shorthaired birddog belly ripped
                        open
                            pink showing
        like red ink paling
                            under a damp sponge
Death at bay a toothpick's prick
        from his blueberry-fat eyes

Mom smearing her middleclass life
with manicured fingers—
*I* knew *this would happen!*

Dad's futile anguish
. . . tears rich as booze

          Buddy whines
                        on barbedwire:
        his mute wound
                        my entrance in . . .
        nothing but gouged works in there

## SPECTRUM ELEGY

*(for Louis Rose)*

A ribbon of violet draped on shoulders, gun
in your lunchbox, cap set straight—you might
have died against metal, filaments of bright steel
arrayed at your chest like blades of shrapnel.
You might have skidded by the hospital
and greeted death with a bomb's quick violence.

Makeshift ghost, you ransacked country roads
in silence intense and deep as indigo
and shuddered the cricket pumpkin dark
with bedsheets flashlit from beneath
as if your demon's breath were lightning! Uncle,
you prankster, did you know the fright you pirated
was treasure rich and inviolate as midnight snow?

The blue of your mechanic's veins
terrified a battery of fingermen who swore
to get you juiced-up and egotripping and raw
with energy until you dared swing an immigrant
Yid fist at America. I loved you because you kicked
fascisti horsemen in the balls and hung
your faith out when the deathwinds blew.

No one ever grew green with desire for you:
you refused to stay planted long enough
and drew your wiry roots out, our soiled imaginings
still clinging, and flew head-on into the first

clean wind. Aerobic and stellar, you broke into
dare-Jesus dancing that clicked like a gun's safety
and jagged a thin lip of tin against time's grain.

I snagged a loop of my soul on your machine,
yellow taxi trafficking in images:
meter down but ticking-off its nickels in your gut
where the true toll was. You rattled away on the crazed
cobbles of the 30's: love-runner and chief itinerant cook—
dishing up whores, caches of cool wine, stashed bread.
At the end of your day's run the dazed guards bellowed.

You were a genius at cards: *Play* this *one!* you'd say,
or *Sit still!* A tease of love and blood, you'd poker-
face it till the flood swept our game away: the world
gone orange suddenly. But we knew your anger was a bluff—
it was the game inside that fooled us, under your mask,
where the cancer waited, then played its ace-high flush
against your round-the-corner straight.

Then the blood came and kept coming, thickly red
and strange. They could do so little. You bled slowly
from my head, thin ribbons of pain. I couldn't hear
what was said when they slipped your body into the bare rip
in the earth like a boy's ruined bicycle. The heat
in my chest brooded like a hen tending a cracked egg.

## DUST FOR BEETLES

*(from the keynote speech at our class reunion)*

. . . you recall, of course, how you amazed
your 4th-grade class by chalking the full
technical name for DDT on the board:
"Where'd ya get the *big* word?" they'd say,
and you'd explain how you got it "offa the bottle—"
how it sat like a jug of lemonade
on the kitchen table; and everyone would go "Yeah!"
being prone to heroes. You used to wear
a Joe DiMaggio T-shirt and had cropped hair
and spent half of each day (before school) crawling,
opossum-like, through spring trees. I remember
that day we wept over the dead possum mother,
her 9 rat-faced babies clinging to her fur
like disciples to a dead Master; how the blood leaked
from her white lips; how we seemed to be falling
off a lean branch into oblivion . . .

It's a bit absurd, now, to think how we clung
to branches, calling to each other over delicately
strung wires, urging miracles—tentatively—upwards
into green leaves. Birds were everywhere, lined up
like refugees—cardinals, orioles, jays:
a bird for every color. I suppose you remember them.

Well, enough! Memories have other purposes. Recall,
instead, how each spring your dad dressed up
in painter's clothes and closed his hand around an opening

nozzle; recall his resolve, under a May noon,
to spray beetles, tent-caterpillars, inchworms out
of existence. Forsythias died into summer
like scorched Aztec maidens, and blueberries
looted from the wood took root and disappointed
no one. And the bugs, for the most part, died
on schedule: Dad piled the dead in heaps to use
as fertilizer for his roses; the roses bloomed,
carefully, intent upon their own preservation.

Only sometimes the damn bugs won
and kept blooming with the roses. I recall
one hot year I wore my arm out smashing beetles
against concrete, drowning them in milk bottles,
racing to other gardens to pursue fresh battles;
they popped like peas under my sneakers, glinting
greenly, briefly, before they died.

Finally, the town took over and saw the job
done right: *DUST FOR BEETLES* became the town motto,
and men were hired to haul the long hoses
that brought the cure for the onslaught
of bugs; and Dad was assured to watch the great trucks
rolling, noisy as dinosaurs, through a thousand streets;
and boys on bikes, charmed by this death-magic, rode blithely
through the white mists like sleighs through snow.

## ANIMA

My sister is alive and beautiful.
Her skeleton sits on a brocaded couch
in Connecticut
instructing neighborhood children.
Her breasts are broad and blue-veined—
an acolyte's white lips pull at each nipple.
The yellow candle in her skull burns
with a soft effulgence
like the dream-auras
in a Chagall painting.
Her finger bones scan nimbly
seeking the perfect navel
in her rural Treblinka.
Her hips encompass Macedonia
and New Haven, Peking and Calcutta.
The smoke of civilization cloaks her shoulders
like a 13th-century mantelletta—the laws
of Solon and Moses flash in that net
like rhinestones.

# COUSIN JERRY

Shakespearean fetus, he
declaimed "To be . . ."
from the womb
                                        and grew
a grotesque red beard and eyes
too wetly blue
and a pocked pallid thorazine-
clammy brow and slug-dull lips
that muddled every song

His body yearned to feel
the back-thrust of a gun:
explosion encased in steel
and guided solely by desire

He demolished armadas of beliefs
after each "Now I lay me . . ."
and slept like a bulldozer and slew,
in dreams, parents who—too well—knew
what was good for him, how he ought
to be

Each day he waylaid
neighborhood children, pressed his ear
to their minds, like a safecracker
listening for jewels

## TO AMY ON WARD 10W

I came to see you on my way back
from the zoo . . .
Your cage was locked,
its thick steel proof
against attack.
Behind the foot-long latch
I heard a sick child laugh,
moan like a snow leopard, and cry
out.
The keyhole was dark and cold
as the face of a spider
crawling toward its kill

*

Your poem cried Out!
*The sun is allowed to* Out!
*through my window, leaves*
*are* Out! *into my body*
*like caterpillars, doom seeps*
Out! *like treacle, I shriek* Out!
*as well as silently. . . .*

*

We never spoke before last Saturday.
I couldn't visualize your face
or your body—rotting flesh of a girl

levitated by fear and drugs
like a fakir on a meat hook.
How still it must be! your intellect
on edge in the immense focused dark,
cocked like a Caesar's thumb

*

Today I came again:
a dude shooting pool said you'd gone
to the beach.
The light over the table was tipped
to pierce eyes,
sliced through my forehead.
I reached for a cue stick.
A nurse materialized
like a godmother.
"You're concealing madness!"
she cried. "Give it here, child!
Deliver!"

*

I stood on the Medicine Line,
stinking of nausea. It was past
Visiting Hours. Piss dripped
in the hallways. No one
would stamp my hand for the trip
out

This morning you escaped
to our child's room: over her crib,
your fat, pocked, fourteen-year-old
face, flabby breasts loose
under linen, jeans flared out
over baggy hips.
Your head bobbed like flotsam,
your thick feet left rubber
on the rug

*

You unscrewed our perfect mornings,
leaked madness from your toes—
a yellow jelly that slowly froze
the space between us.
Under your gaze the sun broke loose,
hung unsocketed:
the juice switched on in you,
pulsed in the soft pad of each finger

Our old fear of too much life hid
from your flaming hands

## FANTASY OVER MY CHILD'S TEARS

Stars are hidden tonight
like answers
from a suicide.
In the conch of our house
my fish-child cries
as if to keep the waters of blue earth
from draining out under her tail.
When I shudder
the air breaks into bubbles
like a tide.

*

In this aquarium
we seem the only fish awake:
she forbids my return
until I have heard the wails
in the other shells.
*Listen objectively*, she scolds,
*try another form . . . something ridiculous*
*. . . a man.*

Her pain rides the wave
of one barbed
hook
and scoops the eyes
from every shark in the world

## A REFUSAL TO ENTER MY FATHER'S SKULL

Your fingers pry me
from the wound,
she is open and red
under me
    held in the flat
    socket of your world
        your smells
singe my body:
all the truth you
give me

*everything I am*
*is spiked with pain*
*unable to lean*
*into the wind*
    *leap upstream*

You dip me
in green flasks
hook me
to tubes intricate
with my blood,
you keep my parts
in laundered sacks
bunched at the whirlpool
    your white technicians
    flap
    sheets in the wind

hurry to machines . . .
she mars your metallic wisdom
widens beneath you:
the way back
is too long

*everything I am*
*sucked like a fat thumb*

Though you break cell walls
memory of rapids
mineral richness of streams
wakes brighter in me
each splash I make
in these shallows
hastens your decay

What races in me is Law,
the image dancing before me
is *Law*
childless, self-contained
I will be shapeless
again
undetectable
will break surface
beyond your stained-glass
brain:
will dance perfectly
and knock upon
no martyrdom

## A FIELD OF GOLDENROD
*(Orient Point, 1975)*

I leave my wife and two young girls behind
and step into a field of goldenrod,
hip-high, throbbing with yellow light.

The soil is white and cracked with run-off brine
that eats down to the roots with a salty flame
fierce and persistent as acetylene.

Lost to my sight, our youngest daughter climbs
the steep ladder welded to the Orient slide.
Near the top step, she forgets to cling, lets go:

her cries rip down through my wife like a lightning bolt.
I stop in my tracks, pinned to the distant beach.
But I'm held by the crop of flowers: each bowing stalk

appears to point the way, spearing an arc
of the cheek-soft sky with its jagged blade.
Each step I take into this field seems free—

the goldenrod is a haven for butterflies.
I bend to see: how still these insects wait!
For them, the path is clear and it leads away.

Behind me, the beach shells break against her face.

## A SIX-POINTED STAR

1

Today you are real, child-to-be.
You kick at the walls of your prison house,
splintering the nerves at the tips
of my fingers—

When I touch my scalp
blood wells up
as if a small taproot
of terror
has become unplugged.

2

I bend over your crib:
you still breathe, yes! yes!
The vaporizer whirrs
like a spaceship,
blows cool wet air—
a kind of invisible ray
potent with the numb murder
of sleep.

Your face is beautiful in the dim light
blowing in from the hallway:
your mouth open so I can see your few teeth,
small bits of your self that will last.
You are the continuance, you make Auschwitz
less of a mockery.

3

Your body is small but perfect,
each pout and dip of flesh
gleaming with soapy water.

When I scrub your limbs
I can see there is hair on them
already, a light down of human
feathers.

You expose yourself so readily
my blood gathers,
throbbing painfully, a thumb
struck by a hammer.

It is all I can handle to towel
you dry.

4

Today in the park
we walked away from your mother:
you ran ahead into the open field,
intent under your snow hood
as the winter sun.

I tossed you the ball under
hand, had to tell you to watch it
fall toward you like a tiny comet:
a dozen times before we could take
our eyes off each other.

5

I push you out again—
already you fly too far
from me, your life rising
quietly from your skull
like hair warming in sunlight.

The swing holds you up
like a gallows, the full weight
of your childhood suspended
on the crosspiece . . .

I push you out again,
watching you drift beyond my reach
on that life raft, pulled back
toward me by your small
gravity.

Each time I push you out
you return more slowly,
with the weight of your bones
towing against you.

6

You brush your hair
little Jew girl—
already the dark roots
flame out,
reach higher with each stroke.

How well you've learned
what I could not teach you:
you wear the star
inside,
ashamed to state too clearly
who you are.

Daughter,
I see the knowledge of pain
guide your soft white arm . . .
your pointed fear
puts out my eyes.

## PUZZLES

Grandfather, twenty years, twenty years
you've waited for this poem—
this magic puzzle I twist into shape,
solder with memory, burnish with speech

Halting old man, shuffling and beat-
down by disenchantment, dulled by poverty
into quiescence, I feared your difference,
your distance, your fragility
breaking out at the high mottled forehead
like a rash
                    You painted houses—
did they paint you? Your brush-callous
was an extra thumb. Your hands were spotted
and your skull: a kind of rose disease
spread by age
                    Who were you, Grandfather?
What was the name you answered to?
On Ellis Island you were merely *Jew*.

You led your brood out of Russia—which town?
What Cossack memories made the trip with you?
Did Colgate Avenue echo with pogroms?
I heard ghost horses gallop when you held me
in your arms
                    Twenty years, Grandfather!
I didn't realize it was so late: those twists
of salvaged wire pulled me toward you

in a way no kiss might do. You were 83
when you died and more of a puzzle to me
than any one you made
                                        Your funeral was the first
I saw: the graveyard was bleak as Leningrad,
the rabbi mumbled into his beard as if he believed
the Czar could hear. The mourners were cloaked
in rain. I wanted you alive, not that puzzle
in the grave
                        Isidor, the hawks are hunting
now: Israel is encased in a bubble of black
gold, the twisted sun-cross appears on sidewalks,
synagogues burn at midnight and at noon. History
reaches into its back pocket, the one marked
*Jew*.
        Grandfather, bombs yearn toward Tel Aviv,
the sheikhs hold torches to the Tablets of the Law,
Africa lifts its fist at Jerusalem. I am running
out of lamb's blood to paint on doors

Come nearer, ghost! Unpuzzle me!

## PORTRAIT WITHOUT A FACE

*(for Jack Fishman,*
*slain by members of the American*
*Nazi Bund—Quarry Pond, Cortlandt,*
*New York, August 17, 1935)*

1
A light swings, lit,
in a brick building—
sways in the gust
of steam boiling up
from the dark street

Four men lean
over a card table,
caps pulled low:
they smoke fear down
to the butt

*Here is the plan . . .*
*shivs and slogans*

*It'll be a picnic!*

2
That weekend they woke
from a two decade rest:
tanks in Watertown
in Cortlandt

Uniforms starched

The Brown Shirts marched
and drilled till dusk

You headed north
to kick in their drum

Did you see Death come
goosestepping
toward you

with jackboots on?

3
In back of the trees
beliefs are staked
to the ground
like prisoners

Each tent flap glows
with a swastika
red as chicken blood

The hard earth
glitters,
bits of glassy mica
in its jaws

4
Below me, the pond flashes

in the August sunlight:
treacherous
and inviting—

I swim through the slough
of decades

Dead fingers
tug me under

You will not be taken!

Your blood will not
be used
to call the old gods
back

The year's death
hurries in your chest
like a last swift falcon

You are up ahead
in the front ranks:
you carry the banner

Leaves catch flame
as you walk

5

You get to the gray tent
first—
your knife goes in

smoothly
like a scalpel

On his soapbox
the *komandir*
growls and frets
like a jackal

*Heil Hitler!*
he sputters

*Heil Hitler!*
intone the rest

You crawl on your belly
but then leap up:
he goes down
into a sunburst
of his own pure blood

6
I walk down
your old turf:
half-demolished buildings
scaffolding
pigeons flying
through chimney necks
bricks blackening
under the moon's acid
touch

Radios on the pavement
squawking *You're next!*
Ph.D.'s hawking hotdogs
old men in cribs
old women hunting
survival
in trash bins

Through broken panes
I watch the light
sway—

Your bones will not stay
buried

I can hear your voice lift
over the night's backed traffic

I climb into this dark room—
it is brighter in here
than outside

7
You are the lost limb
of the amputee:
when it rains
the ghost-nerves scream

If I press my ear
to the earth
I can hear a train

chuffing
on iron tracks

If I lie flat
I can hear
children
mewing like baby seals,
women squealing
as if they've been
impaled,
old men muttering
in wheezy prayer

If I lie flat,
face downwards,
I can hear the time-
bomb
ticking in each car

8

A dog licks my face,
his tongue scours
and chastens

I want to come up
for air
but I can't find
my feet,
I can't touch
bottom

9

Yaakov,
your hand scorches me!

Tell me of the nights
behind curtained windows,
your life radiant—
drawing the hot current
of the age –
adorning you
like a chrysalis
ready to burst

Tell me of the nights
at the edge:
a green field before you
and the urge to run

And the dome of light
at the barricades

10

Broken glass on concrete
voices
unintelligible congregations
behind lit windows

Barbedwire between apartments
electric eyes in flower pots

Encampments

twisted crosses
red patches on black shirts
rifles, stiff spines

A steady hum that shortcircuits
everything

11
A loudspeaker
tracks me down,
announces your doom:
asphyxiation
through drowning
grappling hooks
negligence
communism
careless hands
anger
crushed ribs
protruding rocks
skull fractures
confusion
fascism
meetings
in strange rooms

12
I paint a yellow star
upon your grave,
clear the rubble

I paint at night
working carefully

A dog licks my face
and spills the paint:
enough remains on the brush,
on my fingers

Your blood will not wash
from these quarry stones

## DANCING WITH MY FATHER

1

The road leads down
into a gravel garden
sand orange as a whore's
make-up
slanting down
like the dance floor
of the *Titanic*

We step cautiously
from stone to stone
sinking gradually
into the forbidden
hearing already
the warning notes
under the keel
of the planet

We face each other
and embrace
in silence
touching at last
dancing at last

turning wordlessly
in slow electric
circles
hearing the music
grab inside us

like a steel hand
the strident trumpets
the deep bass purr
of the panther
at the heart
of the world

2

The road leads down
and we go the distance
his beard white and coarse
against my bare shoulder
my eyelids raw against
his salty cheek

We turn against the clock
we dance to the dark tune
the light is blinding

nipple to nipple
his lips lost in my hair

I cling to him
as if he were a ladder

He whispers that his skin
burns
will I soothe him?
I try to peel it off him
my nails cold against
his ribs        like claws

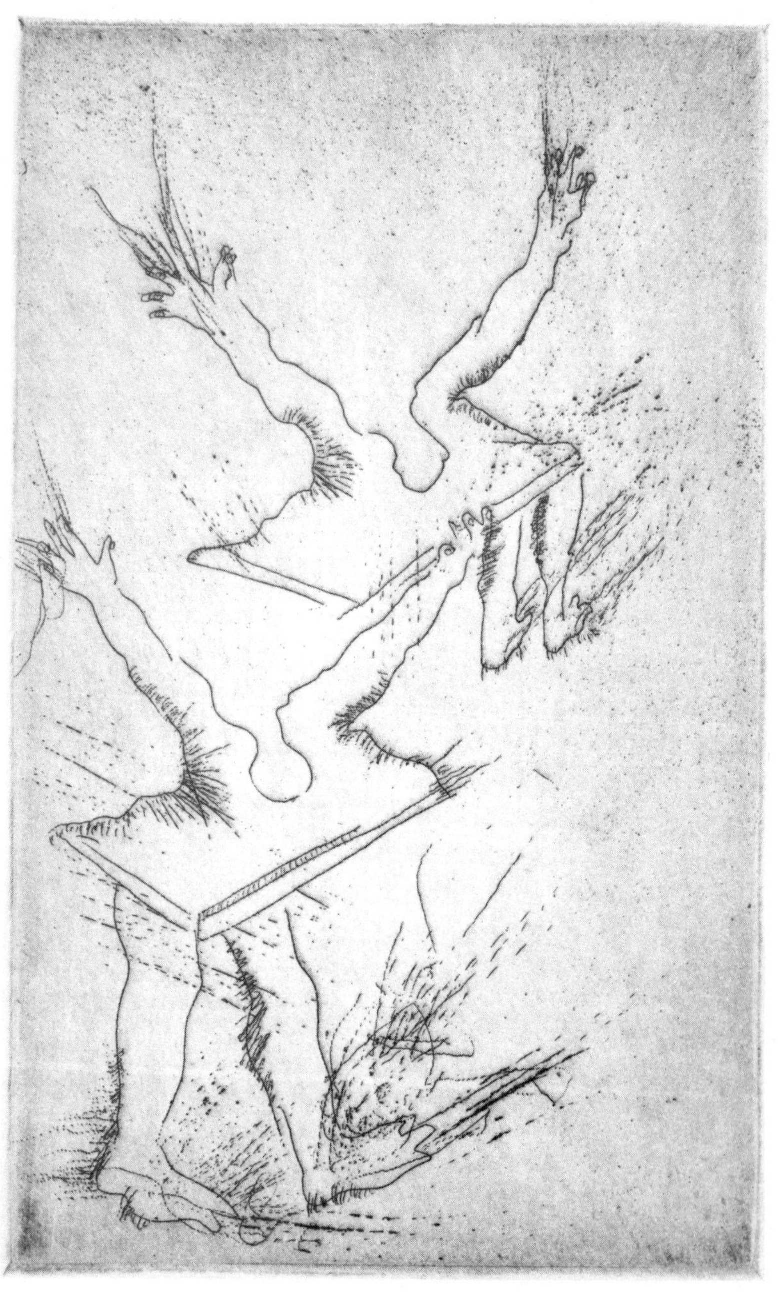

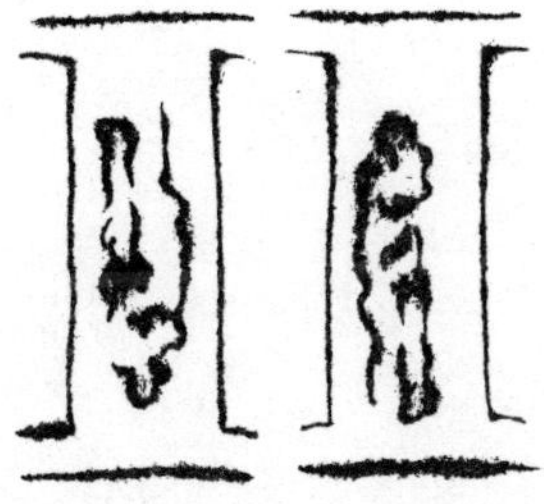

## THE FIRETRUCK

*When books are burnt, humans*
*will be burnt in the end.*
*—Heine*

The firetruck is moving always
through the dimly glaring time-
screen,
red lights *FLASHING*
*FLASHING*
corners of a flag:
the firetruck is coming at me
soundless as a floating coffin,
one blue bulb at its left front fender
potent as a radium capsule
The firemen
are waving at me: black and wet
in monkish slickers,
falling in the brackish darkness:
the firetruck is glowing, gliding
like a hellbound taxi
red as a fish gill
black as a coal vein

*

The firetruck
looms nearer to me
the driver is driven
by a hot bare wire
his hatless head

is bald as a vampire's
*I have no views on saving widows!*
*A body burnt is a seat on the subway!*
His voice is pale as a scar on a baby:
the firetruck is a poor man's abbey
near as the red box in the hallway
*Break the glass and kiss your lady!*
*Crazy! Crazy! Crazy! Crazy!*

*

Rain beads on leaves along the highway:
bright white gleams on translucent pebbles,
wet dead pulsebeats on cooled gravel
                                        inside
my heart holds still as a turtle
The monks chant *Shrivel! Shrivel! Shrivel!*
The sky is white as a mass card

*

Heine knew the world would flame
out under a madman's thumb
                                        and warned
his Jewish countrymen
                                I understand
their numb refusal: *Humdrum! Humdrum!*
In 1821
who knew how well bones could fuse?

## A MORNING AT DACHAU

*But what would Munich be without its lovely*
*surroundings, the rolling hills of Dachau*
*in the northwest. . . .*
*—Munich guidebook, 1966*

In the cellar under Dachau
we found charts and pictures:
charts of extermination
planned as a wedding
or funeral,
pictures of Hitler
and his precise mustache
and his human mind.
1 chart of camps
and 1 of cities taken
and 1 of profit value
in prisoner utilization

Underneath our feet
dank unused stone,
around us silent walls—
bloodless, bloodless

Underneath our feet
blank silent stone,
around us unused pipes
mute as arteries

*

What touched was water
in the dark tunnels:
like the prisoners' urine,
run-off from despair

grief beading pipes
set into cool walls

light fingers resting
on our shoulders

shoes filling small unlit rooms

*

Outside.
30 mass graves tidy as patios

1 late yellow rose
smelling of young girls
who run and make love

## GUIDE ME FROM THIS SAFE HARBOR

*(to Aryeh Lyova Eliav)*

The heroes of our people are not always law-givers
with densely flowing beards and eyes like panthers
or broad-shouldered Samsons groaning under a stone
pantheon of fear. You, Aryeh, are one who has loved
with a silent attentiveness . . . lion with olive branch!
Tonight, I feel your power. I hear the tale of your voyage
beyond the Côte d'Azur, your quest for Zion,
your cargo of abused young women,
eight-hundred of them, Himmler-given,
swept from ruined Belsen,
meant for a blood-price, for the hope of pardon,
set to dreaming in a battered banana boat, with you
for captain—how you deceived the bureaucrats, eluded
the British, weathered the turbulence . . . at last,
were captured, entombed at Cypress, released again.
These Jewish women lived, mothered children,
bore arms, laid brick, cleared and tilled and planted.
Aryeh, lion-heart, I would be with you: almost a heathen
in this rootless land, I have grown soft with bland comforts.
Nothing will be risked while I linger. Tonight,
thought of you pulls me from my safe drift
toward the future. Once more I hunger.

## A DEAD WOMAN ON THE SUBWAY

*The living are dead . . . and the dead live.*
*—Heinrich Boell*

She was waiting as the doors opened,
had been there for years—
locked in space
like bait in a steel trap.

She entered all at once.
Those numbed past waking stirred,
swimming up through the murk of coma
like blind fish drawn to the sun.

We saw the numbers on her arm:
her sickle, her swastika.
A corpse from Belsen.
Gulag stew.

She steamed like horseshit,
teemed like a bag full of germs.
Her face:
A surgeon's mask. A fetal caul.

Her breath seeped like gas.
Her fingers were pure bone.
We gulped her foul musk down
as lights dimmed, brakes screeched.

The lights flashed off and on.
Her wounds refused to close.
Our eyes wouldn't shut.
The fans broke.

Time leaped under the wheels.
Blue lights spat from the dark.
We heard her barbedwire moan.
She took her bandages off.

The train wailed in its cowl.
Picked up speed. Seemed to fall.
We waited in its belly
to be cast up . . .

And smelled fish stiffening
in buckets of salt.
And heard the desperate slap of tails.
And ached for hooks in our jaws.

## AUGUST 12, 1952

*(in memory of 30 Yiddish writers*
*executed under Stalin)*

One month after my 10th birthday
Markish/Kwitko/Bergelson were dead:
men I had no knowledge of. 27 others.
One month after I'd zoomed noisily
through the city   writing no poems
knowing only the little deaths
that could nuzzle in my hand,
Hoffstein/Fefer/Der Nister left
blood on stone. Even if I had known
even if their obituaries had reached me,
had—miraculously—appeared in electro-
luminescent air   even if I'd stumbled
out of my boyhood, become inevitably
human and not merely grown, nothing
could be done. There was no time
to fabricate superman out of my prayers
no time to save the novels   poems
stashed incautiously in cupboards   no
time to stop their remarkable bones
from walking away from them: Markish/
Kwitko/Bergelson. I had to climb up
18 years to hear their names.

## DEATH MARCH

Not the numbers    but the sound—
murmurs in the singlefile crowds
flickering windy candles,
not the place    but the names
marked on placards hung
from living necks—
to be tolled to the cameras
for a visual kaddish,
not the hour    but the clear darkness
through which mourners    like monks
in 14th-century habits    passed the shrine—
the great doomed Capitol
Taj Mahal
sepulchre of the dead Prince: Justice.

Each of us one of the silent dead
returned to march through the white city
past white TV lamps holding white candles
past the White House in our white bones,
a parade of resurrected soldiers—
bearers of ghost guns and phantom armor
decked with blood medals and chevrons of flesh
garlanded with the black hungers
of our enemies—
camouflaged as war protesters
bearing our constitutional wounds
in silent wonder
along a treadmill through hell.

## NOVEMBER, 1970
*Charjabber, East Pakistan*

A child flung into his grave
takes too much with him:
rest         termination
bits of cloth.

An official mourns:
*The dead should get*
*nothing.*

## SONG FOR THE RELIEF COPTERS

In the morning
after no one has slept
in the paddies
in the mist
in the heat
with the dead
who lie eaten
by the storm
in the photo
in the paper
after we've eaten
and slept peacefully
in each other's arms,
the helicopters come
like a squadron
of gods
like a huge wind
like a wave breaking
in our blood

## YOUR DREAM

*(for W. D. Ehrhart: Vietnam, 1967-1968)*

Your dream is my poem,
this blade of glass that nicks me
as we talk: partying
with friends
till a gang breaks in
alien, helmeted, violent,
without rage:
shooting Sue Burns where she crawls
and brays,
getting Davey Wilks with his hands
on his skull—wasting them all,
but leaving you whole.

Your dream is the mirror that hangs
on my wall.

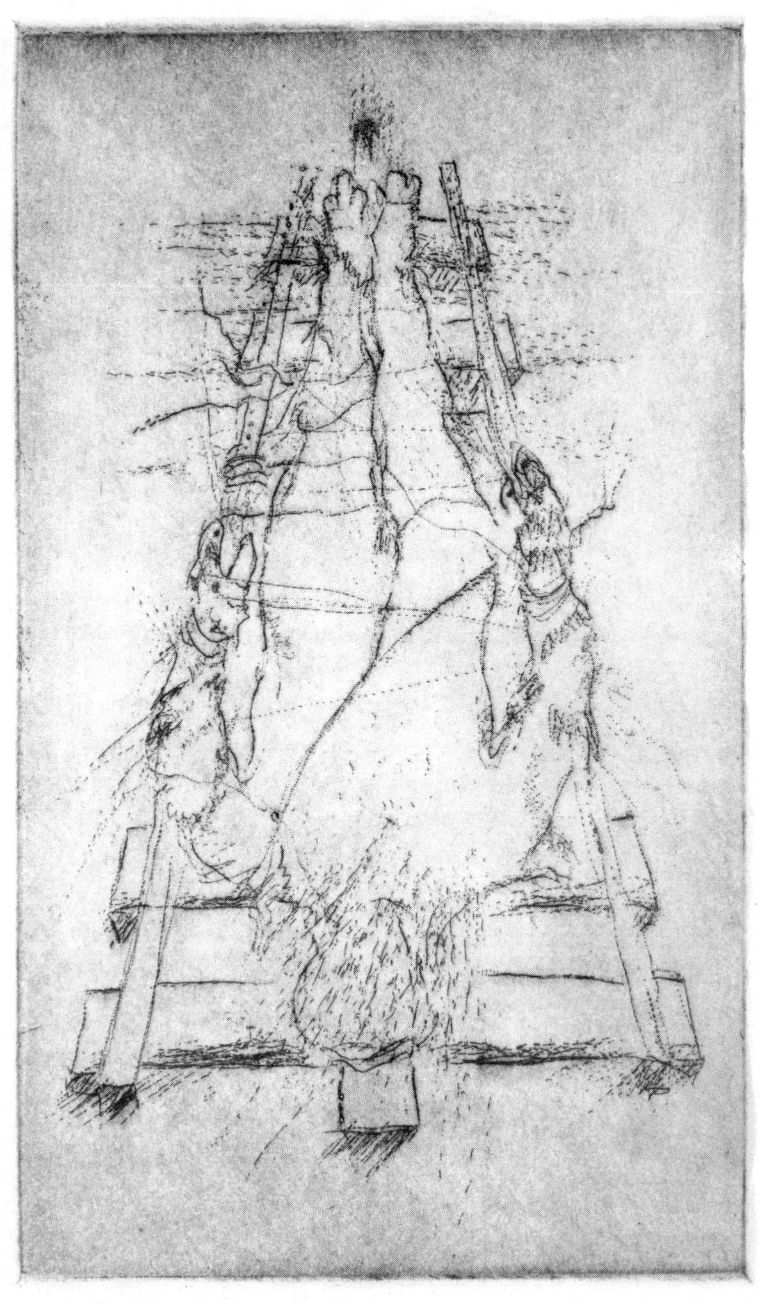

## THE COMMUTER

Sam sits next to me on the train,
butterfly blue pinstripe suit creased
across the groin, shoes scuffed over
the toes. When the conductor shuffles
through his ritual, Sam loosens the hitch-
knot bunched at his throat.
                                        "Look,"
he says. "Wha wouldja do if ya wife came
to bed naked as a cow? Twenty-five years
that woman's worn nightgowns!"
                                                Sam's
a nice guy. Never smells bad, doesn't talk
much (usually), buys the *NEWS* each morning
so I get to read it when he falls asleep
at Rockville Centre. What am I supposed to do?
I can see the rusty sign announcing *PASCO FENCES*.
Bales of reinforced wire sprawl on the gravel.
Redwood boards weather in the offshore drizzle.
Weeds are shrunken, parched to a frazzle.
I've been over this route longer than I'd care
to tell.
            "Listen," he starts again. "It's no
skin off my nose . . . but then she goes
an laughs. *Everything with you's gotta be*
serious. *You come home steamin. When*
*supper's late, it's a big* tragedy. *If*
*you got locked in the house without ya goddam*
*TV, y'd think it was jail. This family*

*means nothin to ya. Why don'tcha just up
an leave!*
What now?"

His damp hands are smearing ink on the paper.
Concrete and glass clickclack by. Appearances
breaking in. Cars hurrying to keep up, keep up.
Across the aisle a young kid keeps her hand
in her friend's lap. Her breasts are real
under her sweater. I wonder if she sleeps raw,
takes his sperm in her mouth.
Sam is quiet
and sunk into his seat the rest of the voyage.
His chest heaves at each station, breath thin
through his nostrils. I read quickly through
familiar columns: lies. Guys like Sam
tied to the third rail.

## WHAT'S LEFT AFTER A GOOD WOMAN DIES?

*(for Ray Gill: in memoriam, Eileen Gill)*

After her death, the silence chills.
You live. You manage. Night falls,
cracking and shattering, like ice melting
in a ruined hive. Her voice, recalled,
hides the insistent clamor of other lives.

The bed is glacial stone. This is where
she lived, lay close to you, as to no other.
Forty years. You lie back, shivering.

Frail ghosts. Siberian landscapes.
This dream of relief. These icicles.
Nothing in this house warms.

## OLD MAN

On his front lawn an old man is talking
to himself, trying to keep his hand in life,
needing to feel it burn, needing to see the skin
peel back—but nothing's taking. He stands

talking to himself about himself like a car
stalled on the tracks. His body is dead
already, but he can't accept it: he leaks
luke warm tea . . .
his pantleg is soaked
with it. I want to rush up to him and shake
him, to screech into his face like a child
feeding a tantrum, to forget myself enough
to say what I mean.

## OLD WOMEN

*Vus iz geven iz geven*

Old women slip from car seats, stiff as mannequins,
in blue bat night, the hour of lost children.
*Thud, thud, upon the pavement.*

The veins of the cracking sky are black with cold blood
and the clot of sun rubber-masks light.
*Oy! Oy! Oy! scream the buttons.*

One splinters as she falls, the chipped head revolving
a slow palette, dust hues, on macadam.
*Thud, thud, upon the pavement.*

Out of the seam in her skull a bright pink flurry
floats like a faceless ghost, oohing softly.
*Oy! Oy! Oy! scream the buttons.*

It's a sash from Tobruk—a fear-torn banner,
flash of heroics—of an old order.
*Silk flutterings, and the sighs.*

A second figurehead rolls by, her thighs creaking:
yes, she recalls the rough crossing, the fog.
*Oh! what will become of us?*

The gold around her breasts like cheddar cheese flaking
her salmon hair splitting, her wormed heart food.
*Time has eaten our babies.*

Her chest is tacked with medals, martyr's ware, steel
buttons etched in Yiddish. And each mouth cries
*Oh! what will become of us?*

*We are old, we have fed our children, our husbands*
*lie in cold beds below the ivy. Oh!*
*Time has eaten our babies.*

The words spill from the wound in her back, like bibles:
black, rectangular words—they have decked walls.
*Silk flutterings*, *and the sighs.*

The third would have been an actress: she bears the script
between her fingers, a ticker-tape scroll.
*Oy! Oy! Oy! scream the buttons.*

It, too, bares words—burnt offerings—names from the past
to prove the glories: *CLASS DANCER. CLASS CLOWN.*
*Oh! what will become of us?*

The stiff joints fail, the ribbon ravels. Oh! lady—
your garnished wood, your mothering, your star.
*Oy! Oy! Oy! scream the buttons.*

Ah! those splendid moments! Silk flutterings, the sighs.
The shiny Rolls Royce days. The slow falling.
*Thud, thud, upon the pavement.*

## BUNGALOW PEOPLE

Bungalow people
Old-World-aged
other-tongued
stare
from scabbing porches,
kibitz, knit—
perpetually—
emblems of desire:
shawls to mourn in,
bibs for the newly born.

When I walk past them
to pluck
the sacred mushroom
curiosity
they sigh audibly
and knit faster.

I feel their angry wind
butt my legs
like a goat:
nothing scares me
like their death-
scratched voices.

Nothing muffles the horn
in my side
blowing pain.

I can't get away
from the burning porches,
from their white-hot
needles
weaving up the sun:
the more sweat I pour
into leaving
the nearer they come.

## A HISTORY LESSON
*(for Mildred Plumb: antiquary)*

The woman behind the door
is unexpected

a green fir tree
inside a tomb:

"I'm *old* Connecticut," she
tells me, "12 generations

buried together."

Like the weathered graves
of New London

(mourning sea captains
lost off St. Martin

or virtuous wives of
landlocked sailors)

she is old-world
never to be recaptured

skin polished with
experience of people

like handcarved cooking
bowls and homemade pewter

her hands utensils
that have scoured granite

and peeled birch fibers
for a broom

and caressed the dark
grain of wood

till it gleamed

*

In the child's room she
imagines young boys

adventure—a spool that
winds    unwinds
between them

presences
but not ghosts:
she is all this
history has to offer

(her flesh

against the beams
does not rest
or touch them)
she has seen

the moon and sun
rise
over the coals
in the chimney
like departing
birds

*

In Joshua Hempsted's
diary (she explains)
one reads momentous

trivia:
of years with no summers
and winters that were green

and how to carve a chest
for squirreling the
soul's desires

how Arnold fledged his guns
with scarlet and burned
the green jasper land

of New London—
how the days
fanned out like leaves

of basil and sweet thyme
(shrunk to a frazzle
now, nothing furious

or splendid with
defeat)
how things change

against most perfect
schedules

*

In this dominion
of curios
she wears the light
like an earring

the heirloomed past
like a cameo
at her breast.

## BLACK HORSE OF NIGHT, RETURN
*(after Lorca's "Song of the Rider")*

Black horse of night, return
Enter this castle
Whinny and gaze up at the nameless stars

These walls are fables
and only the soul is left, faceless
in the silence of the planets

Wild stallion,
your unshod hoofbeats startle
the drunken pilgrims stalled here

in all manner of costly apparel
Outside, in the country
you come from, a labyrinth of black streets

are bathed in your shadows
that sweep across the faces of sleepwalkers
who sway in the unbridled darkness

as if they are balanced on cables
bolted to the bells of cathedrals . . .
Black horse,

*¿Dónde llevas tu jinete muerto?*
For too long, you could be seen
only in the distance, in glimpses,

prancing
and pawing the earth, bearing your burden
of death, the black moon's bloody bandit

Now you approach, again, your shining body
pulling against the reins, the pure silver
of your eyes hammering at my spirit

*¿Dónde . . . muerto?: Where to with your dead rider?*

## THE ICE POETS

All night it whispers
and collects, enclosing
each bud in a clear bauble,
sheathing branch and twig,
weighing down centuries
of growth.

Everything shimmers
and reflects: it is
a landscape made wholly
ghostly—given to suspension,
not death.

Blades of dried grass
are locked in patterns
precise as firing squads
aiming into the dark.

Each seed pod seems
a crystal ball
pure enough to yield truth.

Ice orders sleep: almost all
obey . . . in darkened rooms
only machines stay awake—

But we remain outside
letting doors shut forever:

needing to prove our faith,
affirming an old allegiance—
and the ice sings to us,
*Demon! First love! My own*
*true self! I make the universe*
*still for you—this once.*

## GHOSTS CRY OUT

Everything we love is taken from us:
the wooded hide-outs of our childhoods,
the nights of eerie shadows we named *Wolf King,*
*Emperor Bat, Drunken Sadie, Witch's Hat—*
the friends we gave our lives to with no holding back,
who led us upstream through thickets and bracken
and over moss-slick rocks
and into trouble and out of boredom
and left no tracks

They are all bulldozed, unrecognizable

And the adults who nurtured us, who listened—
they fill the graveyards

Each day we are brutalized: the Ice hastens
We live among strangers who slaughter their infants
The rulers survive—our heroes are slain or broken
We see only death, the earth ripped open
like the soft furred belly of a cornered fox

The wars come in waves: everything we love is pulled
beyond our holding . . .
Our parents go down beneath the cold blindfolds of water
Our children drown under the crashing blackjacks of surf

Ghosts cry out for the green blood of the earth

Printed April 1977 at the Print Center, Inc. Cover, illustrations and design by Coco Gordon. Composing and lay-out by Charles Fishman. General hard work, advice and encouragement donated by Beverly Lawn, George William Fisher and Coco Gordon, with assistance from Mildred Jeffrey, Tom Carbone, Barry Paikoff, and Peter Hood. There are 1000 copies in this First Edition. A limited number have been handbound in leatherette by Nikkels Bookbinding and Gold Stamping, of which 50 have been signed and numbered by the poet.

Cover design done with drypoint on plexiglass, with type in Caslon 36 pt. and Caslon 24 pt. italic. Special thanks to Donn Steward for printing Coco's three etched illustrations.

photo by Barry Paikoff

Charles Fishman was born July 10, 1942 in Freeport, New York, but lived in the Bronx until he was eight. Since then, he has resided in suburban Long Island, where he now lives with his wife, his two daughters, his cat, and his organic garden. Fishman is co-editor of *XANADU* and teaches at the State University of New York at Farmingdale. His poetry has been published in periodicals as diverse as *GHOST DANCE* and *SALMAGUNDI*, *SNOWY EGRET* and *KANSAS QUARTERLY*, *POETRY NOW* and *THE NEW YORK TIMES*.